91 Tips on Selling Today

Paul Jensen

Books by the same author:

The Joy of Having Puppies
(with Vibeke Jensen)
Available at www.lulu.com/pauljensen

The Small Munsterlander
A Breed Apart
(with Don Knaus)
Available at www.lulu.com/pauljensen

Could Young Love Be a Metaphor for Your Business Success
Marketing Made Memorable
Available at
www.amazon.com/dp/B00HB97HM2

Preparing Your Product for Exporting
Available at http://amzn.to/1aLXsZq

Copyright © 2014 Paul Jensen All Rights Reserved

Introduction

What is selling?
Selling is the art of convincing an individual or a group that employment of your products or services are necessary to their own success.

The tips in this book have not been placed in any particular order. I have written them down the way they came to me as I was writing this book. They all have their place and importance in the business of selling. And selling is everybody's job today.

The book is not meant to be read cover to cover in one sitting, but rather to be used as a workbook where you only read one tip a day and write your notes at the bottom of each page. So keep it at your desk and in a 3 months' time you will have preserved to memory the 91 tips on selling.

Go get them tiger!

I would like to start the book with a couple of quotes from a great salesman and author, namely Zig Ziglar.

You can get everything in life you want if you will just help enough other people get what they want.
Zig Ziglar

If you are selling a legitimate product that solves a problem and you sell it at a fair price, the customer makes the best deal.
Zig Ziglar

Tip 1
Don't learn the tricks of the trade – learn the trade.

Notes
_____
_____
_____
_____

Tip 2
People don't care how much you know as long as they don't know how much you care.
   Show empathy.

Notes

_____
_____
_____
_____

Tip 3
The most important part of the sales process is the sales person.
> First impressions are important; your customers will see you and make assumptions about you even before you speak, and will carry those visual impressions away to remember long after they forget what you said.

Notes

_____
_____
_____
_____

Tip 4
Get the customers smiling

If you can get the customers smiling as you go through the body of your presentation, your chances of closing the sale is considerably greater.

A friendly smile is a reasonable good indicator that they are buying you as a person and will therefore be more likely to buy what you are selling.

Notes

_____
_____
_____

Tip 5
The customer is always right

I grew up where my Mom had a corner grocery store. As an eight-year old lad I would help my Mom by weighing off 1 and 2 pounds of sugar, flour etc. and while doing so I would often hear the conversations in the store. Afterwards I would ask Mom why she didn't correct the customer because even I know he/she was wrong. My Mom's response always was: "The customer is always right."

Notes
_____
_____
_____
_____

Tip 6
Products sell faster if customers can touch them

This one is another from my Mom. Whenever we had a product that was on a shelf behind the counter and it didn't sell Mom placed it on the counter and within two days it was all gone. Her understanding of human behavior is on display in all the supermarkets of today.

Notes
_____
_____
_____
_____

Tip 7
Selling is a skill
     Selling is not an innate. I have at times believed that since I have been selling all my life but had it not been for the education I got from my Mom I probably would be no better at selling than an untrained person.
     Nobody comes out of the womb a star sales person or a great golf player.

Notes
_____
_____
_____
_____

Tip 8
Be a good listener
Listening allows you to get accurate feedback Get out there where the rubber meets the road and talk to customers. I remember one sales professional telling me that he had listened himself into more sales than he had talked his way into.

Notes
_____
_____
_____
_____

Tip 9
Ask open ended questions
> What do you want to achieve?
> What do you want to avoid?
> Who makes the decision?
> How do they make the decision?
> Is there a budget available for this project?
> What else can I offer you?
> When do you expect a decision to be made?

Notes

_____
_____
_____
_____

Tip 10
Be aware of your body language
  Scientists have determined that only 7% of our communication comes from the spoken word, the way we say it is 38% and the majority 55% from our body language.

Notes
_____
_____
_____
_____

Tip 11
Put yourself in the buyer's shoes
    Look at your business through the eyes of your customer.
    Good selling starts with getting information about the customer's pain.

Notes
_____
_____
_____
_____

Tip 12
Be a problem solver
   Customers are not buying things – they are looking for solutions to their problems.

Notes
_____
_____
_____
_____

Tip 13
Be ready to walk away
Walk away when you realize you don't belong.

Notes

_____
_____
_____
_____

Tip 14
Use heart selling

During a recent interview I did with Eric Lofholm regarding his book: *TheSystem* he mentioned HEART selling which Zig Ziglar has also defined as:

H in the heart of your sales career is *honesty*.

E is *ego* and *empathy*.

A is your *attitude* towards you, your prospects, and profession.

R is for physical, mental and spiritual *reserve*.

T is for *tough* – and the toughest thing is love.

Notes
_____
_____
_____
_____

Tip 15
Develop a selling system
    Develop and follow a lead generation method.
    Set appointments.
    Convert leads to buyers.

Notes
_____
_____
_____
_____

Tip 16
You need to understand the customer

Give customers whatever they want, how they want it, when they want it, wherever they want it.

Do whatever it takes to create happy, delighted satisfied customers.

Remember the customer signs everybody's check.

Do you know that Harvey Mackay of *'Swim with the Sharks'* fame has developed a 66-question profile called "Mackay 66" of all his customers?

Notes

_____
_____
_____

Tip 17

Be perceived as similar to the customer
If the customer moves forward in the chair, do the same but not overtly though.

Notes

_____
_____
_____
_____

Tip 18
Selling equals service
When it comes to service, little things don't mean a lot. They mean everything.

Notes
_____
_____
_____
_____

Tip 19
Don't discount your services
Discounting undermines the value of your offerings.

Notes
___
___
___
___

Tip 20
Be authentic
    Be yourself, don't act the part; be the part.

Notes
___
___
___
___

Tip 21
Make it easy for the customer to buy
    Sell the products or services the customer wants and needs.

Notes
_____
_____
_____
_____

Tip 22
You can't sell if there is no room in the budget
   You cannot get blood from a stone.

Notes
_____
_____
_____
_____

Tip 23
It is easier to sell to a current customer than to develop a new one

Much of the time spent cracking new accounts would produce more results if it were applied to getting more business from your present customers.

Notes
_____
_____
_____
_____

Tip 24
Spend time with decision makers
Always try to get as high up in the organization as possible.

Notes
_____
_____
_____
_____

Tip 25
Ask for introductions not referrals
Introductions require more effort on the part of the customer so coach them.

Notes
_____
_____
_____
_____

Tip 26
Turn point-of-sale into a subscription service

If your product or service lends itself to this it is a good deal for both you and the customers.

Notes
_____
_____
_____
_____

Tip 27
Network with potential customers
　　Don't go to your professional association meetings go to the customer's association meetings and make presentations and be introduced by your existing customers.

Notes
_____
_____
_____
_____

Tip 28
Be prepared
   Be knowledgeable about your product or service but don't preach it. Have the knowledge available to answer any questions or objections a customer may have.

Notes
_____
_____
_____

Tip 29
Be clear on what problem your products solve

Your knowledge about your product should be so clear that you know exactly what pain your product or service can limit or eliminate.

Notes

_____
_____
_____
_____

Tip 30
Develop trust with your customer
Always treat the customer with respect, follow his lead, don't waste time, be light-hearted together if that is called for.

Notes
_____
_____
_____
_____

Tip 31
Be original
   A strategy that depends on a commodity mentality can be deadly.

Notes
_____
_____
_____
_____

Tip 32
Be responsible
>If it is to be it is up to me.
>I can handle this.
>It's worth my time and effort.

Notes
___
___
___
___

Tip 33
Be likable
You'll do more business if people like you.
People prefer to do business with those they like, trust, admire and respect.

Notes
_____
_____
_____
_____

Tip 34
Be a service fanatic
   Great service isn't the product of doing anything a thousand percent better. It comes from doing thousand of things one percent better.

Notes
_____
_____
_____
_____

Tip 35
See yourself as a winner
(See Dennis Waitley: *The Psychology of Winning*)

Winning is all in the attitude.
Positive self-esteem is one of the most important and basic qualities of a winning person.
Winners take full responsibility for determining their actions in their own lives.
Winners know that life is a self-fulfilling prophesy, that a person usually gets what he or she actively expects, or as the Chinese say: if you plant beans you will reap beans; if you plant corn you will reap corn.

Notes
_____
_____
_____
_____

Tip 36
Your product should improve your customer's situation
Satisfied customers will provide the loyalty, higher sales, and profits that will boost your satisfaction (and company's satisfaction).

Notes
___
___
___
___

Tip 37
Look the customer in the eyes (but don't stare)

The eyes are the pathways to a person's soul.

If you are not making eye contact, the message you are sending is that you are not trustworthy.

Notes
_____
_____
_____
_____

Tip 38
Respect your customer's time
   Most customers value time more than money.

Notes
_____
_____
_____
_____

Tip 39
Be on time for an appointment
　　Being on time is late. Be there at least 10 minutes early.

Notes

_____
_____
_____
_____

Tip 40
Be willing to be quiet
> There may be a reason while we have two ears and only one mouth.
> It allows you to think more and think creatively.

Notes
_____
_____
_____
_____

Tip 41
Use modern technology in your business
The world we live in today offers us so many avenues of communication with our customers that you need to be up on what your customers are using and follow them.

Notes

_____
_____
_____
_____

Tip 42
Never be defensive
If anything you say is taken the wrong way, try to explain it another way and explain you didn't mean any disrespect.

Notes
_____
_____
_____
_____

Tip 43
Keep in touch with your customers
    Keep nurturing without being obnoxious.

Notes
_____
_____
_____
_____

Tip 44
Don't badmouth the competition
   Walk around any suggestions from anybody to comments on a competitor as the cat walks around the hot porridge.

Notes
_____
_____
_____
_____

Tip 45

Learn to pronounce your customer's name

Many people you come in contact with have peculiar names so ask how the name is pronounced and make a real effort in learning the right pronunciation. Very few people make that effort – so you will be seen as special.

Notes

_____
_____
_____
_____

Tip 46
Remember your business cards
   Do I need to say any more?
   A sales person without business cards is naked.

Notes

_____
_____
_____
_____

Tip 47
Understand the reason for a customer not buying

There are five reasons people will not buy from you. These are:
No need
No money
No hurry
No Desire
No trust.
The last reason kills more deals than the others combined!

Notes
_____
_____
_____
_____

Tip 48
Become a professional sales person
>Believe in your product.
Believe in yourself.
Work on your timing.
Develop a sense of humor.
Realize that what the customer wants isn't necessarily what he's telling you.

Notes
___
___
___
___

Tip 49
Make only sincere compliments
    Don't ever be a fake.

Notes
_____
_____
_____
_____

Tip 50
Use positive and warm words when selling
Words like: understand, proven, health, easy, guarantee, safety, save, love, comfort, proud, profit, deserve, happy, value, fun, good taste, gracious.

Notes
_____
_____
_____
_____

Tip 51
Use your customer's name
There is no sweeter sound than ones name on someone else's lips.

Notes
_____
_____
_____
_____

Tip 52
Be enthused about selling
   Having and showing a positive attitude in your presentation is contagious. Enthusiasm comes from Greek, meaning "filled with the spirit of God."

Notes
_____
_____
_____
_____

Tip 53
Keep Selling

The only difference between a big shot and a little shot is – the big shot is just a little shot who kept on shooting.

Follow up until they buy or die!
Eric Lofholm

Notes
_____
_____
_____
_____

Tip 54
Maintain a healthy self-image
Your self-image is important, so build a good one and you will be able to build your sales career bigger, better, and faster.

Notes
_____
_____
_____
_____

Tip 55
Don't become emotional
> You'll loose your capacity to deal effectively.
> Don't take anything personally.
> Your feelings don't matter in business.

Notes

_____
_____
_____
_____

Tip 56
Set selling goals
   Set number of leads on a daily/weekly basis.
   Appointments daily/weekly.
   Number or Customers daily/weekly.

Notes
_____
_____
_____
_____

Tip 57
Find role models

Do you remember the story about Bannister? The first person to run a mile under 4 minutes. Until that time people believed that it was not humanly possible.

Shortly after many runners have broken the 4-minute time barrier. Bannister had shown the way.

Do you have any role models you can emulate?

Notes
_____
_____
_____
_____

Tip 58
Keep studying selling by reading good books

If you think education is expensive, just look at the cost of ignorance. In the last 90 days, how many books have you read?

In the last 12 months. how many classes have you attended to improve your selling skills?

Notes
_____
_____
_____

Tip 59
Be enthusiastic
　　Nothing of consequence was ever achieved without enthusiasm.
　　Do what you love and love what you do.

Notes
_____
_____
_____
_____

Tip 60
Smile
> Smiles don't cost anything and pays big dividends. It makes you feel good and it makes the recipient feel good.
> Confident, successful people smile.
> Smiles convey self-acceptance and an accepting attitude towards others.
> Smiles inspire confidence in the person who is smiling.
> Smiles boost the confidence of the person who sees the smile

Notes
_____
_____
_____
_____

Tip 61
If you loose a sale ask for feedback
This is the best way to better your hit rate.

Notes
_____
_____
_____
_____

Tip 62
People buy for their reason
>You succeed to the extent that you learn what your customer need and find a superior way to deliver it.

Notes
___
___
___
___

Tip 63
More things are bought on emotion than logic

Be passionate about your products or services.

When dealing with people, remember you are not dealing with creatures of logic, but with creatures of emotion.
　　　Dale Carnegie: *Public Speaking*

Notes
_____
_____
_____
_____

Tip 64
People hate to be sold, but they love to buy
    Place yourself in the customer's shoes.

Notes
_____
_____
_____
_____

Tip 65
Your sales goal should be a satisfied customer
    Be results oriented.

Notes
_____
_____
_____
_____

Tip 66
You are not selling goods and services you are selling value
> The customer is willing to pay for value – the greatest combination of quality and service.

Notes
_____
_____
_____
_____

Tip 67
People prefer to do business with people they like, trust, admire and respect
   Do everything you can to become that person.

Notes
_____
_____
_____
_____

Tip 68
People will do business with the ones they OWE, NEED, OR LIKE.
>The ones they owe they will work with once.
>The ones they need they will work with maybe only once.
>The ones they like they will continue to work with.

Notes
_____
_____
_____
_____

Tip 69
Telephones are not for selling
    Just get the appointment.

Notes
_____
_____
_____
_____

Tip 70
Differentiate
>Be different. Find a way to present yourself, your products or services that make them memorable.

Notes
___
___
___
___

Tip 71
There is nothing lost and much to be gained by admitting that you're human

    Admitting what you don't know immediately puts those you are dealing with at ease.

    Conceding an error is always a sign of strength.

    Admit your mistakes as soon as you notice them.

    Accept that you are not perfect.

Notes
_____
_____
_____
_____

Tip 72
Show more interest in your customers than the competition
Mail a thank you letter to your customer after making the sale.

Notes
_____
_____
_____
_____

Tip 73
Have empathy
Become a nurturer of your customers
If all you have is ego you will be likely to make shortcuts, make misrepresentations and exaggerations that eventually will catch up to you. Look at the products and services you sell through the customer's eyes. That's empathy – and that's selling the professional way.

Notes

_____
_____
_____
_____

Tip 74
Paraphrase
> Briefly summarize substantial questions or comments in your own words. Make sure you understand the customer's concern.

Notes
_____
_____
_____
_____

Tip 75
Ask for the sale
> Don't loose the impact of a great presentation by not asking for the sale. Sales trainer Chris Hegarty says that 63% of all sales interviews end with no specific invitation to buy!

Notes
_____
_____
_____
_____

Tip 76
Learn all you can – don't tell all you know.
    Be a life-long learner.

Notes
_____
_____
_____
_____

Tip 77
Develop basic personal values
   I like people.
   I feel good about myself.
   I am motivated by challenge more than money.
   I like solving problems.
   I don't have to win every time.

Notes
_____
_____
_____
_____

Tip 78
Don't make promises you cannot keep
    Don't oversell. You'll invariable loose.
    And don't make omissions.

Notes

_____
_____
_____
_____

Tip 79
Learn to use humor
    Humor breaks down barriers.
    Humor helps people forgive more easily, it breaks tension.
    Humor keeps things from getting boring.

Notes
_____
_____
_____
_____

Tip 80
Show respect for customer's opinions
Recognize that good manners and grace are always in style.

Notes
_____
_____
_____
_____

Tip 81
Remember to close

Each close you use should give the prospect a reason to buy, an excuse for buying, or information so that he can intelligently act in his own best interest.

Sales trainer John Hammond has successfully handled price objections with this close:
"If there were a way I could show you that the price is more than fair and the product is worth every dime we're asking, would you go ahead and take advantage of our offer today?"

Notes
_____
_____
_____
_____

Tip 82
Be honest
You've got to believe. Honesty means that you believe so deeply, so completely, so fervently in what you are selling that you can't understand why the prospect is not buying.
Not only should you believe in the product or service you sell but you should also believe in and be loyal to the company you represent.

Notes
_____
_____
_____
_____

Tip 83
Speak plainly
    Say what you mean, just as you think it. Don't try to impress anyone. Be direct. Don't worry about who likes or doesn't like what you have to say.

Notes
_____
_____
_____
_____

Tip 84
Beware of first impressions
    Great sales people are aware that first impressions are powerful and create lasting attitudes. They understand that interpersonal relationships can be won or lost in about the first four minutes of a conversation.

Notes
_____
_____
_____
_____

Tip 85
Appearance

The way you look at the outside has a definite bearing on how you feel and see yourself on the inside.

I served in the military as a platoon leader and 1st lieutenant and I was determined to be perfect in appearance since my 30+ men had 100% of their time to inspect me while I on the average only had 3% of my time to inspect each of them. I had to look the way the men expected an officer to look.

Notes

_____
_____
_____
_____

Tip 86
Show them

You can't simply tell people how great you are. You have to show them. They have to (sometimes literally) see for themselves.

A picture is worth a thousand words. Remember that people are learning through three channels, auditory, visual and kinesthetic. All three channels are touched when you are showing and telling.

Notes
_____
_____
_____
_____

Tip 87
Tell a story that relates to your product or service

We have been conditioned since childhood to listen to stories. We learn from them and they entertain us.

Notes
_____
_____
_____
_____

Tip 88
Ask rhetorical questions
   Questions that starts with: "What if you …. (it forces the old (or reptilian) brain to focus on finding an answer, it gets the buyer engaged).

Notes
_____
_____
_____
_____

Tip 89
Always be courteous
    Remember to say Thank You

Notes
_____
_____
_____
_____

Tip 90
Don't sweat the small stuff
You're going to die some day, everything else is small stuff.
Les Brown

Notes
_____
_____
_____
_____

Tip 91
Have persistence

Nothing in the world can take the place of persistence. Talent will not; nothing is more common than unsuccessful men with talent. Genius will not; unrewarded genius is almost a proverb. Education will not; the world is full of educated derelicts. Persistence and determination alone are omnipotent.

      Calvin Coolidge

Notes
_____
_____
_____
_____

Resources

Zig Ziglar
Zig Ziglar's Secrets of Closing the Sale
http://www.amazon.com/gp/product/0425081028

Zig Ziglar
See You At The Top: 25th Anniversary Edition
http://www.amazon.com/gp/product/0743596781

Eric Lofholm
The System
http://tinyurl.com/kb9r8t4

Nicholas A.C. Read
Selling to the C-Suite: What Every Executive Wants You to Know About Successfully Selling to the Top
http://miniurl.com/j9mE

Neil Rackham
SPIN Selling
http://miniurl.com/6yVB

Jeff Shore
Be Bold and Win the Sale: Get Out of Your Comfort Zone and Boost Your Performance, with a foreword by Mark Sanborn, New York Times bestselling author of The Fred Factor
http://www.amazon.com/gp/product/0071829229

Harvey Mackay
The Mackay MBA of Selling in the Real World
http://tinyurl.com/mtb28qa

About the Author

Mr. Paul Jensen's business career of 40 plus years includes experience in a family owned contracting firm, a materials' laboratory, consulting engineering firms, business development, and international trade.

Mr. Jensen has worked in operations, management, sales and marketing, and strategic planning.

In 1970 Mr. Jensen and family immigrated to the United States where he spent the next 20 years with the Cambridge consulting firm of Bolt Beranek and Newman Inc. While there he held many positions from purely technical manager to business leader with P&L responsibility of $5M to $7 M.

During the past 20 plus years Mr. Jensen has been involved in various aspects of consulting both in the US and overseas.

International achievements include opening trade relations between the Czech Republic and Taiwan and developing environmentally progressive commercial fishing fleets for 3rd world countries.

Mr. Jensen has also developed a training course for the Italian company of Pirelli and continued on-the-job training over a three-year period.

In addition Mr. Jensen has performed consulting work in Austria, Brazil, Canada, Denmark, Norway, and Turkey. Mr. Jensen has conducted business negotiations in Costa Rica, Hong Kong, Kenya, The Philippines, Czech Republic, Russia, Trinidad and Tobago, Taiwan, Ukraine, and United Arab Emirates.

Mr. Jensen has recently established himself as an independent consulting practice under the name of Center for International Market Affairs, Inc. serving small business clients.

M. Jensen's formal education includes a Master of Science Degree in Civil and Structural Engineering from the Technical University of Denmark. In the US he has taken post graduate courses in Marketing, Management, Negotiations, Technical Writing, Communication, Decision Making, Selling, Public Speaking, Industrial Hygiene, and Robotics.

Mr. Jensen is the founder of the Small Munsterlander Club of North America, a breed club for this German originated bird dog.

In his spare time Mr. Jensen enjoys working with his dogs and cooking.